Chapter 1 – Jonah 1:1-3 7

Chapter 2 – Jonah 1:4-7 13

Chapter 3 – Jonah 1:8-12 26

Chapter 4 – Jonah 1:13-17 34

Sermon Outline #1 – Jonah 1:1-17 42

Chapter 5 – Jonah 2:1-7 43

Chapter 6 – Jonah 2:8-10 50

Sermon Outline #2 – Jonah 2:1-10 55

Chapter 7 – Jonah 3:1-4 56

Chapter 8 – Jonah 3:5-10 64

Sermon Outline #3 – Jonah 3:1-10 75

Chapter 9 – Jonah 4:1-4 76

Chapter 10 – Jonah 4:5-11 84

Sermon Outline #4 – Jonah 4:1-11 100

Chapter 1 – Jonah 1:1-3

1.Now the word of the Lord came unto Jonah the Son of Amittai, saying. 2. Arise, go to Nineveh, that great city, and cry against it; for their wickedness is come up before me. But Jonah rose up to flee unto Tarshish from the presence of the Lord, and went down to Joppa; and he found a ship going to Tarshish: so he paid the fare thereof, and went down into it, to go with them unto Tarshish from the presence of the Lord.

The Book of Jonah begins with the Word of God. This is where all great movements of God begin. In the beginning, God spoke and creation came into being. Before she gave birth to our Lord, Mary obeyed the Word of the Lord by stating: "…Behold the handmaid of the Lord; be it unto me according to thy word…." (Luke 1:38) We Methodist Christians are a people of one book, the Bible, the Word of God. We are under Scripture, and we believe Scripture is the primary criterion through which all theological truth is viewed and interpreted. In the Wesleyan movement, we call this the primacy of Scripture, and we hold that all theological truth must be viewed and analyzed through the lens of the Bible. Therefore, the story of Jonah begins in a place familiar to all Christians. The story begins with the Word of the Lord.

The Word of the Lord

Notice that verse 1 tells us that "…the word of the Lord came unto Jonah…" Jonah is called to be God's prophet through the Word of God. God still calls women and men to be his prophets through the Bible. I was converted while reading the Bible, and I was called to preach as I read the Bible. The Word of the Lord still comes into the lives of persons and inspires them to say "yes" to God. In 2 Timothy 3:16-17, we read that:

> All scripture is given by inspiration of God, and is profitable for doctrine, for reproof, for correction, for instruction in righteousness: That the man of God may be perfect, throughly furnished unto all good works.

When God calls us to do great things for him and for the expansion of his Son's kingdom, he oftentimes calls and equips us through his Word. We see this in the story of Jonah, and the first thing this great book points out is what we Methodist Christians call the primacy of Scripture as we read that the Word of the Lord came to Jonah.

The Two Ways to Rise

The Bible is clear in both the Old and New Testaments that there are two ways women and men can respond to God's call, teachings, and instructions. We can rise to obey God, or we can rise to disobey God. Usually, there is no "gray" area, and to ride the fence is to disobey. The Scriptures also consistently point out that the person who consistently rises to disobey will encounter trials, difficulty, despair, and death. However, those who consistently rise to obey God and God's Word will experience blessings, joy, peace, and life. Indeed, difficult times are a reality in the lives of all people including those who live for and obey God. The difference is that obedient Christians knows that their suffering and trials have a greater purpose, and these trials are not chastisement or a correcting measure for their sins. The trials of the obedient Christian are within God's watchful care and serve to strengthen and empower us to answer God's call and share God's Word with the world.

As we begin our study of the Book of Jonah, we see that Jonah responds to the Word of the Lord, and he rises in response to the Word. However, he rises to disobey instead of to obey. Verse 3 says "…Jonah rose up to flee unto Tarshish from the presence of the Lord,…" Jonah rises to flee. He rises to run away from God and God's call on his life. This is the crucial mistake that many women and men still make today. They choose themselves, sin, the world, and the idols of the world, instead of choosing and obeying God. This is idolatry and blatant disobedience to God, and it is breaking First Commandment: "Thou shalt have no other gods before me" (Exodus 20:3). This kind of disobedience to God, and the Word of God, puts the Christian in a place where God must chastise and correct him or her. We certainly see this in the story of Jonah as the great storm confronts the ship and Jonah is thrown into the ocean.

This also reminds us of the great faithfulness of God. He loves us too much to just let us go our own way when we choose the weak and worthless idols of this world over his power, his Word, his glory, and his kingdom. Just as God loved Jonah too much than to just let him run off to Tarshish, he loves us too much than to just let us choose this world and its ways over his. By his amazing grace, God comes to us, and he chastises and corrects us, and he guides us back onto the "…the paths of righteousness for his name's sake" (Psalm 23:3).

The Grace of God

We can never run so far away from God that we are out of reach of his grace. All of my life, I have heard about the long arm of the law. This is the idea that law enforcement has an amazing and mysterious ability to catch criminals even when there is a great geographical or time difference between the criminal and his or her crime. The long arm of the law can reach across time and space to find the guilty party and bring them to justice. God's grace is like this too. I call it the long arm of the Lord. In the story of Jonah, we are reminded that God's grace can come into any area of our lives and rescue, redeem, renew, strengthening us with hope, purpose, and giving us a second chance. Indeed, the Book of Jonah is about our God who is a God of second, third, and fourth chances. God is always at work rescuing us from ourselves and setting us on that straight path that leads to life, joy, and peace. Jonah's story reminds us of that great truth Paul proclaims in Romans 5:20 where he states: "…where sin abounded, grace did much more abound."

There is no place to which a man or woman can fall where the amazing and wonderful grace of almighty God cannot find, lift up, redeem, and restore them. Indeed, the God we learn about in the Book of Jonah is the God of the second chance and the God of the two hundred and twenty-second chance. And, since God never gives up on us, we should never give up on one another. As Christians, we should always be willing to give our brother or sister in Christ a second chance if he or she sins against us.

Chapter 2 – Jonah 1:4-7

4. But the Lord sent out a great wind into the sea, and there was a mighty tempest in the sea, so that the ship was like to be broken. 5. Then the mariners were afraid, and cried every man unto his god, and cast forth the wares that were in the ship into the sea, to lighten it of them. But Jonah was gone down into the sides of the ship; and he lay, and was fast asleep. 6. So the shipmaster came to him, and said unto him, What meanest thou, O sleeper? arise, call upon thy God, if so be that God will think upon us, that we perish not. 7. And they said every one to his fellow, Come, and let us cast lots, that we may know for whose cause this evil is upon us. So they cast lots, and the lot fell upon Jonah.

In these verses, we see several more great theological truths. The first thing we see is that the wind and the storm are "sent" by God. The storm God sends has a divine purpose, and it is a double-edged sword. Firstly, the storm comes upon the ship as a consequence of Jonah's sin of disobeying God and evading God's call for him to preach repentance to the Ninevites. However, the storm is also an avenue of God's grace as it begins the series of events that will bring Jonah back into fellowship with God and that sweet place that living for the Lord brings to those who obey him. This points to the sovereignty of God, and it reminds us that nothing happens in our lives that is out of God's control and benevolent care. In Verse 3, we saw that when Jonah arrived in Joppa, "he" found a ship going to Tarshish. However, Jonah didn't find the storm; the storm found him. In his amazing grace and love, God "sent" the wind and the storm which inaugurates Jonah's return to his God.

God Is Glorified Even In our Disobedience

Here, we see that others are watching us in our relationship with God. We are witnesses, and we set an example. In his disobedience, Jonah is setting a poor example. We can either be good examples of what a Christian is and does, or we can be poor examples. The sailors on the ship know that the dangerous wind and the mighty storm are the results of Jonah displeasing his God. This demonstrates to the sailors God's power and strength, and they see that Jonah's God commands even the winds and the waves. As Christians, we know that the winds and the waves obey our Lord Jesus Christ. After Jesus calms the storm in the great story in Matthew 8:23-28, we read that

"...the men marveled, saying, What manner of man is this, that even the winds and the sea obey him?" (Matthew 8:27)

We also see that our interactions with our God can prompt either religious devotion or worldly sinfulness in others. We have more of an impact on those around us than we realize. The sailors and their captain know that the storm is judgment sent to Jonah by his God, and many of them begin praying to their gods asking that they not perish amid the mighty wind and the tempestuous waves. Even disobedient and unsaved sinners, as well as pagan idolaters, can sometimes see when God is disciplining and correcting us. God is glorified in this, and the trials in our lives that come from God's chastening and discipline frequently are an avenue of God's grace in our lives. God is so loving, merciful, and good that even when he disciplines us, his chastening is rooted and grounded in his grace and love. The storms that we face in life, which are many, oftentimes are literally the hand of God as he "sends" the storms so we will recognize that we are on the wrong path. We can then repent and turn away from the sin in our lives and get back on track with God.

Repentance and Renewal

Repentance is a very important aspect of Christian discipleship, and the apostle John makes this very clear in 1 John 1:9 where he states: "If we confess our sins, he is faithful and just to forgive us of our sins, and to cleanse us from all unrighteousness." We don't just repent once when we accept Christ, but we repent periodically as we complete our Christian journey. When we realize we have sinned, we need to repent. Repentance involves "confessing" our sins. In other words, we agree with what God says about the sin in our lives, and we acknowledge and agree with God that the sin is wrong by turning away from it and forsaking it. Where there is this true repentance, God forgives and he cleanses. Oftentimes, Christians will only repent when their sins have brought a great storm into their lives. If the storms and difficulties in our lives lead us back to God, we know that the storm very well may have been "sent" to us by our loving heavenly Father so that we could be reminded that the way of disobedience is not the way we want to go. The way we want to go is the way of obedience and faith that gets us back on the same page with God where we can reach our full potential in his kingdom. So, in the Book of Jonah, we see that Jonah is both a poor example and a good example. This is true for us as well, and persons around us see when God disciplines us, and they see when God blesses and rewards us. When we obey God and live for him by loving God and each other, we are good examples and our light shines before others to the glory of God. This is what Jesus speaks of in Matthew 5:16 where he proclaims: "Let your light shine before men, that they may see your good works, and glorify your Father which is in heaven."

Hiding From Our God Who Finds Us

In verse 5, we see that "… Jonah was gone down into the sides of the ship; and he lay, and was fast asleep." Here, Jonah is attempting to hide from God. Jonah knows that the ship is being tossed about in the tempest as a result of his running away from and disobeying God. Sometimes, when we Christians are disobeying God, we don't want to read our Bibles, attend church, or pray. This is because we know we are not pleasing God.

Although one of the most basic truths about God is that nothing is hidden from him, the old adage that you can run but you can't hide is relevant here. Jonah knows deep down that he cannot hide from God and the consequences of his sins. Nevertheless, he goes down into the side of the ship where he doesn't have to look at and acknowledge the storm God "sent" as judgment and discipline for his blatant disobedience. Here, Jonah is much like the Ostrich with his head in the sand. We can try to escape the consequences of our sins by sleeping, drinking, overeating, shopping, or hiding, but the fact that God sees all is a simple theological truth that is both disquieting and comforting. It disturbs us when we think that God sees all of our sins, but it also holds true that God sees all of our good works and obedience. The fact that God sees and rewards our obedience to his Word and Commandments is a great comfort and inspires us to obey just as the fact that he sees and allows consequences for our sins should prompt us to consistently say "no" to sin and "yes" to God. When we obey and live for God, our lives become a "living sacrifice" to God. The apostle Paul points this out in Romans 12:1-2 where he states:

> I beseech you therefore, brethren, by the mercies of God, that ye present your bodies a living sacrifice, holy, acceptable unto God, which is your reasonable service. And be not conformed to this world: but be ye transformed by the renewing of your mind, that ye may prove what is that good, and acceptable, and perfect, will of God.

Here, Paul points out that it is only "reasonable" that we obey and live for God in light of all that he has done for us in and through the life, death, and resurrection of his Son our Lord. Bloody sacrifices for our sins are no longer necessary since the blood of Christ shed at the cross was the once-and-for-all sacrifice for our sins. (See Hebrews 9-10) Therefore, we are now called to be "living sacrifices" by living our lives for God and consistently obeying God by loving God and each other. Sleeping down is the side of the ship, trying to hide from God, Jonah is not reaching his full potential for God. At this point, he is not living the holy life that his God has called and equipped him to live. He is not using his gifts to preach repentance to the Ninevites. On the contrary, he is hiding in the lower part of the ship, and this highlights the fact that we will find ourselves in the lower places in the world if we disobey God and try to run and hide from him. God called Jonah to do something great, but Jonah decides to go his own way. He finds himself in a predicament as he realizes his disobedience has brought dire circumstances to him and the crew of the ship.

The Captain Finds Jonah

Jonah is confronted about his disobedience by the captain of the ship who may or may not be a holy man. This reminds us that our disobedience to God is seen not only by other Christians, but it is seen by those who don't follow or believe in Jesus. Sin is seen by others, and God will sometimes use unbelievers to confront us and convict us of our sins. In the case of Jonah, the captain of the ship comes to Jonah and says: "...What meanest thou, O sleeper? arise, call upon thy God, if so be that God will think upon us, that we perish not" (V. 6). Notice that the captain tells Jonah to "arise." Indeed, even the captain, who is probably not religious, points to the possibility of a second chance, and he points to the power of prayer. He also points to the possibility that God will be merciful if Jonah will approach his God in prayer and plead for mercy. Indeed, God promises this to us in 2 Chronicles 7:14 where we read: "If my people, which are called by my name, shall humble themselves, and pray, and seek my face, and turn from their wicked ways; then will I hear from heaven, and will forgive their sin, and will heal their land." The captain is correct that God will show mercy if Jonah will "arise" and call out to him in repentance and prayer.

Repentance is something that God always recognizes and rewards. With God, as with our fellow women and men, talk is cheap and actions speak louder than words. We can say that we are sorry for our sins and that we repent; however, words mean very little if they aren't backed up by action. True repentance involves "turning away" from our sins and walking in the opposite direction which is in the direction of holiness and righteousness. Here, as the captain approaches Jonah hiding down in the sides of the ship, God speaks through the captain who tells Jonah to "arise." Jonah is to "arise" to righteousness instead of disobedience, and he is being given a second chance to answer the call of God on his life. God gives us second and third and fourth chances also, and we need to learn from our mistakes, forsake our sins, and make every effort to do God's will in our lives.

Being Pure in Heart

The Scriptures make it very clear that if we want to obey God, and we are willing to do the hard work involved in true discipleship, God will guide us, help us, and walk along with us in our journey. In Matthew 5:8, Jesus says: "Blessed are the pure on heart; for they shall see God." Indeed, we grow in holiness as we get closer to God, and we grow closer to God as we eliminate the sin in our hearts and lives. This allows us a closer walk with the Lord, and our lights shine brighter for him as we become more like him. We Methodist Christians call this Sanctifying Grace, and it is the grace that we grow in as we grow in holiness. As he is confronted by the captain, Jonah is made very aware of his sin of running from and disobeying God. Similarly, the Holy Spirit will confront any true Christian who is disobeying God. Then, the Christian has a choice. He or she can repent and "arise" to righteousness, or he or she can refuse to repent which is the equivalent of "arising" to disobedience.

The captain even believes that, if Jonah will repent and obey "his" God, God will be merciful and the storm will cease, and the ship will not be destroyed. The arrival of and confrontation brought about by the captain reminds us that we cannot hide from God when we disobey. God knows where we are, and this is something we celebrate and rejoice in when we are living our lives in obedience and righteousness. Indeed, God is always with us, and he never leaves nor forsakes us. (Matthew 28:20, Hebrews 13:5) This simple theological truth strengthens and empowers us to face any fear and overcome any obstacle. The obedient Christian is like a one man or one woman army, and he or she cannot be conquered or defeated. Indeed, the obedient Christian who kneels before Jesus Christ can stand before anyone, and he or she can "...do all things through Christ which strengtheneth..." (Philippians 4:13) him or her.

Holiness and the joy of living in a close relationship with God is reserved for those who are willing to do the hard work of Christian discipleship. Jonah ran from God's call because he didn't like the Ninevites, but he also didn't want to do the hard work involved in walking with and serving God. Jonah wanted to do things his way, and we can see that his way involves running, hiding, being scared, and refusing to take responsibility. Jonah is not answering and obeying God's call on his life, and the result is that he is not living up to his full potential. When we don't obey God, and live for him, we miss out on who we could be and who God has called us to be. However, the good news is that it is never too late to follow Jonah's good example by repenting, changing directions, and getting back on track with God. When we do, we will find that God hasn't moved, and he's right there where he was when we left to go our own stubborn way.

Chapter 3 – Jonah 1:8-12

8. Then said they unto him, Tell us, we pray thee, for whose cause this evil is upon us; What is thine occupation? And whence comest thou? What is thy country? And of what people art thou? 9. And he said unto them, I am an Hebrew; and I fear the Lord, and the God of heaven, which hath made the sea and the dry land. 10. Then were the men exceedingly afraid, and said unto him, Why hast thou done this? For the men knew that he fled from the presence of the Lord, because he had told them. 11. Then said they unto him, What shall we do unto thee; that the sea may be calm unto us? For the sea wrought and was tempestuous. 12. And he said unto them, Take me up, and cast me forth into the sea; so shall the sea be calm unto you: for I know that for my sake this great tempest is upon you.

In these verses, we see a powerful truth. We cannot hide from who we are. Jonah is not only running from God. He is also running from himself. Although we can sometimes buy into the false idea that we can run from God and our responsibilities in his kingdom, we can never even create the illusion of running from ourselves. Mirrors abound in our culture, and we prepare for our days in front of one every morning. Similarly, the man or woman looking back at us in the mirror is oftentimes one of the last persons we see before retiring at night. Indeed, we can run from God, and we can sometimes even sell ourselves on the fact that we have eluded him. However, we can't even pretend to run from ourselves. Our inner critic is the one judge we cannot escape, and he or she can sometimes be brutally forthright and blunt. We oftentimes show great amounts of mercy and forgiveness to others remembering that Jesus teaches us: "Blessed are the merciful: for they shall obtain mercy" (Matthew 5:7). However, we frequently do not extend such mercy and kindness to ourselves. We judge ourselves with unyielding criticism and precision.

This, however, can be a good thing, and we see that it is a good thing in the story of Jonah. He has successfully eluded God's call, and he is on a ship headed to Tarshish. He is successfully travelling away from Nineveh which is the place God has called him to go to and preach repentance and forgiveness. His escape appears to be a success until we realize that there is one religious Jew that cannot be escaped. He cannot escape the man of God, who loves God, and serves God; he cannot escape the critical and discerning eye of God's man, the prophet Jonah. This is good news for the

Christian living in the contemporary world today also. We may be able to evade our responsibilities to God, others, and the church. However, we can never escape from ourselves. We must answer to ourselves. We celebrate this because in answering to ourselves, we answer to our God who created us, saved us, called us, and equipped us to do great things and to be strong servants of our Lord and Savior, Jesus Christ. Indeed, sometimes our eyes are the eyes of the Lord, and our self-critical corrections are the discipline and chastening of our loving God.

Jonah Confronts Jonah

The crew cast lots in order to determine who is the cause of the great calamity that has come upon them, and the lot falls upon Jonah. Then, they ask Jonah who he is and why this terrible storm has come as judgment upon him and the ship. Jonah responds, and his response gives us one of the most powerful verses of Scripture in the entire Book of Jonah as Jonah emphatically states: "...I am an Hebrew; and I fear the Lord, the God of heaven, which hath made the sea and the dry land" (V. 9). This is the beginning of Jonah's rehabilitation. Repentance involves claiming who we are in Christ and living up to our potential in the kingdom of God. We will do well to remember the words of St. Paul in 2 Corinthians 5:17 where he states: "…if any man be in Christ, he is a new creature: old things are passed away; behold, all things are become new." Because Jonah is a man of God, he is not able to evade God completely because he cannot evade himself. As God's man, and God's servant, Jonah himself will exact God's judgment for his sins. God does not have to speak from the whirlwind telling the crew to cast Jonah into the sea. On the contrary, God doesn't have to speak at all because Jonah begins doing his job as a prophet by speaking God's message to the people at the proper time. Jonah communicates God's message in Verse 12 where he proclaims: "…Take me up, and cast me forth into the sea; so shall the sea be calm unto you: for I know that for my sake this great tempest is upon you."

The Man of God Emerges

In this section of the book, Jonah comes to himself much as the Prodigal Son did when he found himself broke and feeding the pigs in a foreign land. (Luke 15:11-32) He is unable to run from the reality that he is a man of God who has been called by God to preach to the Ninevites. Jonah also knows that the innocent members of the crew of the ship are in peril, and they may never see their families again because of Jonah's disobedience to God. Here, we see the man of God emerge. Jonah exacts his own judgment because the religious man that he is is very concerned about the safety of the men on this ship who are completely "not guilty" of the crime that brought this horrific storm to the ship. Theological arguments pointing out original sin and the sinfulness of all human beings are of no interest to Jonah, the man of God, who accepts God's judgment like a man. He doesn't play the blame game, but he takes the blame upon himself. He announces judgment upon himself, and the crew does as he requests and casts him into the sea. The man who boarded the ship was running from God and himself, but the man who is thrown off of the ship is Jonah, the Hebrew Prophet, called to speak for God and proclaim repentance and forgiveness to the people of Nineveh. Indeed, the moment of his judgment has become one of his finest moments as he takes responsibility for his sins and willingly answers to his God who "...made the sea and the dry land" (V. 9).

Judgment and Grace

This brings us to one of the most prominent themes in the Book of Jonah, and it is that even God's judgment and chastening are avenues of his love and grace. In Psalm 101:1, the Psalmist proclaims: "I will sing of mercy and judgment: unto thee, O Lord, will I sing." Here, the Psalmist sings praises to the Lord not only for his "mercy" but also for his "judgment." The correction of the Lord in the life of the Christian is a manifestation of God's grace because it oftentimes prompts repentance, renewal, and a new commitment to living for and answering God's call. Those who have been given second, third, and fourth chances are frequently willing to go the distance for God by doing great things for God that others wouldn't do. The role of martyrs for Christ, who willingly gave their lives for their Lord, is filled with ordinary Christian women and men who had been given second, third, and two hundred and twenty-third chances by God. Indeed, Jonah's God, our God, is a God who believes in and offers second chances, and many times the second chance begins with God's judgment which leads to conviction, repentance, and renewal.

In 1 John 4:7-8, the apostle John says:

> Beloved, let us love one another; for love is of God; and every one that loveth is born of God; and knoweth God. He that loveth not knoweth not God; for God is love.

Here, we see that God is love. Therefore, God is always loving us even when he is disciplining and correcting us. We Evangelical Christians like to say to one another that: "God is good!" Then, our sister or brother in the Lord will say: "All the time!" Then, we respond: "All the time!" and our sister or brother responds: "God is good!" We celebrate our faith by greeting one another with these familiar words, but it is important that we remember what it is we are actually saying. We are saying that our God is always good and doing something good, and this includes those days and seasons in our lives when things don't seem to go our way. This also includes those times when God convicts us of sins, and we are prompted to repent and to renew our commitment to God. Because God is love, everything he does in our lives is rooted and grounded in his grace, and this includes his discipline and correction. Jonah's judgment begins with him being thrown from the ship, and it continues with the arrival of the big fish. All of this originates in God's grace and love as Jonah is given a second chance through these awesome events. God does the same thing in our lives. He loves us too much to let us go our own way, and he orchestrates events so we will be brought back to where we need to be in our lives. Those given second and third chances should obey the words of Jesus in Matthew 3:8 where he says: "Bring forth therefore fruits meet for repentance." Indeed, "God is good"…"all the time"…"all the time"…."God is good."

Chapter 4 – Jonah 1:13-17

13. Nevertheless the men rowed hard to bring it to the land; but they could not: for the sea wrought, and was tempestuous against them. 14. Wherefore they cried unto the Lord, and said, We beseech thee, let us not perish for this man's life, and lay not upon us innocent blood: for thou, O Lord, has done as it pleased thee. 15. So they took up Jonah, and cast him forth into the sea: and the sea ceased from her raging. 16. Then the men feared the Lord exceedingly, and offered a sacrifice unto the Lord, and made vows. 17. Now the Lord had prepared a great fish to swallow up Jonah. And Jonah was in the belly of the fish three days and three nights.

We have several interesting truths in these verses. We see that the crew of the ship tried to save Jonah. Perhaps they admired his religious devotion, and his willingness to take responsibility for the storm. Jonah may have expressed concern and care for the men of the crew, and they appreciated his concern for their safety. When they are unable to bring the ship to safety, the men of the ship toss Jonah into the sea, and the sea immediately calms down. Perhaps this prompts religious devotion in the men of the ship because they have witnessed God's interactions with his prophet. This highlights the fact that we are always witnessing to others, and God is even glorified by our negative example when we disobey. Even when we disobey and refuse to do God's will, others are confronted with the reality that God exists when they see him convict, chastise, discipline, and correct us.

God Is Glorified as Jonah Is Judged

God's judgment of Jonah begins with the storm, and this brings about his being cast into the sea. Then, a great fish which God "prepared" comes along and swallows Jonah. God's judgment upon Jonah is his being cast into the sea. The mariners already know that God is judging Jonah, so the reality of God has already been highlighted among these sailors on this troubled ship. However, when the precise judgment of God is exacted upon God's disobedient servant, God's power and presence on the ship becomes indisputable, and the sailors begin to worship Jonah's God. In Verses 15-16, we read:

> So they took up Jonah, and cast him forth into the sea: and the sea ceased from her raging. Then the men feared the Lord exceedingly,

and offered a sacrifice unto the Lord, and made vows.

It is important that we note the exact timing of the religious devotion of the sailors. It occurs when the sea immediately becomes calm as Jonah is tossed into it. This reminds us that unbelievers and other Christians are impacted by our witness. They see when God blesses us for obedience, and they see when God disciplines us for our disobedience. While being disobedient and running from God, the prophet Jonah is still able to lead people to God even though it is through God's revealing himself in Jonah's judgment. This points to the magnificence of God and his dominion and reign over all the earth and over all circumstances. This reminds us that: "For as the heavens are higher than the earth, so are [God's] ways higher than [our] ways, and [God's] thoughts than [our] thoughts" (Isaiah 55:9). And, this also reminds us: "…that all things work together for good to them that love [him], to them who are the called according to his purpose" (Romans 8:28). Indeed,

God and his amazing grace are greater and bigger than all of our sins

The Great Fish

With the arrival of the great fish, we see that God's grace is still at work in the midst of judgment. Jonah has been thrown into the ocean as judgment for his sin of running from and disobeying God, and he is suppose to be overcome by the water and drown. However, God still loves Jonah, and God wants Jonah to have a second chance. God sends a great fish to swallow Jonah. Indeed, the fact that the fish consumes Jonah prompts us to identify the fish as a continuation of God's judgment. Indeed, this may be true since the fish's access to Jonah is a direct result of him being hurled into the sea. However, we need to make sure we recognize that the fish also becomes the vessel, a sort of submarine, provided by God's amazing grace that Jonah rides to safety.

In Verse 17, we read: "Now the Lord had prepared a great fish to swallow up Jonah. And Jonah was in the belly of the fish three days and three nights." Although Jesus identifies the great fish as a whale in Matthew 12:40, the writer of the Book of Jonah doesn't tell us much about the fish. However, we are told one very important thing. We are told that the Lord "prepared" the fish. This means God has designed, enabled, equipped, and sent this particular fish to do this particular thing at this exact time. The fish has been called and equipped by God to provide Jonah safe and certain transportation out "…of the valley of the shadow of death…" (Psalm 23:4) and onto dry land. This reminds us that God's grace, mercy, and deliverance can show up in the most unexpected places and by unsuspecting circumstances. Certainly, if we were eyewitnesses to the fish swallowing the prophet, we would be making Jonah's funeral arrangements. It is very unlikely that we would view the fish's consuming of the prophet as anything other than the end of the road for him. However, we are dealing with the God of miracles, wonder, and amazing grace. Jonah's end is a new beginning, and his severe chastisement leads him to a second chance to get right with God and to do God's will. Indeed, the fact that the great fish saves Jonah from the sea reminds us that St. Paul is correct in Ephesians 3:20 where he proclaims that God: "…is able to do exceeding abundantly above all that we ask or think, according to the power that worketh in us."

The Sign of Jonah

After he is swallowed by the fish, Jonah is in the fish's belly for three days and three nights. In Matthew 12:38-42, we have the Scribes and Pharisees asking Jesus for a sign, and Jesus tells them:

> …An evil and adulterous generation seeketh after a sign; and there shall no sign be given to it, but the sign of the prophet Jonas: For as Jonas was three days and three nights in the whale's belly; so shall the Son of man be three days and three nights in the heart of the earth. The men of Nineveh shall rise in judgment with this generation, and shall condemn it: because they repented at the preaching of Jonas; and, behold, a greater than Jonas is here. The queen of the south shall rise up in judgment with this generation, and shall condemn it: for she came from the uttermost parts of the earth to hear the wisdom of Solomon; and behold, a greater than Solomon is here.

Jesus is rebuking the Scribes and Pharisees for requiring a "sign," and he tells them that the only sign there will be is the "sign of Jonah." Jesus wasn't impressed with the lack of faith and blatant hypocrisy he observed among many of the Scribes and Pharisees. Jesus explains clearly that he will be placed in the earth for three days and three nights just as Jonah was in the belly of the great fish for three days and three nights.

The Gospel Story, the Good News, that Jesus the Christ, the promised Messiah, has died on the cross for sinners, atoned for their sins, been buried, and arose on the third day is the Sign of Jonah. Jesus calls it the Sign of Jonah because it takes great faith to believe that Jonah could be swallowed by a whale, spend three days and three nights in this realm of darkness and utter abandonment, and then emerge victorious on dry land on the third day. Similarly, it takes great faith to believe that God would come and walk among us in the Jewish flesh of the Messiah, be rejected by his own people, be sentenced to death like a criminal, be subjected to the most horrific form of capital punishment in the ancient world, die, be buried in a tomb, and rise in power and glory on the third day. Persons are to repent and believe when they see the Sign of Jonah, and it is the Gospel Story presented through the preaching of the church. Persons can repent, believe the Gospel, and be saved, or they can claim it is just as impossible for Jesus to have risen from the dead as it was for a man to survive three days and three nights in belly of a whale and emerge alive and well on dry land. If they believe the latter, they will miss the Good News and die in their sins. However, those who truly repent of their sins and believe the Gospel will receive everlasting life in the kingdom of heaven with their Savior who died, arose, and will come again. Indeed, we love the Sign of Jonah and proclaim it in the Eucharistic Liturgy of the church when we proclaim together that: "Christ has died; Christ is risen; Christ will come again."

Sermon Outline #1 – Jonah 1:1-17

Title: "When God Pursues, Finds, and Forgives Us"
Theme: God's Amazing Grace, Mercy, Love, and
　　　Forgiveness

1. Verses 1-3 -- Like Jonah, we too sometimes run from God and God's call.

    A. Romans 5:8 -- God still loves us.

    B. Romans 5:20 – God's grace abounds.

2. Verses 4-7 -- God's grace reaches us, confronts us, corrects us, and saves us, and we are given another chance to walk with God.

    A. God's grace in the judgment of Jonah in the storm and the fish.

    B. Isaiah 55:9. Romans 8:28 – God works all things together for good like the storm and the fish.

3. Verses 15-17 -- Just as God's grace saved Jonah from drowning in the Sea and suffocating in the fish, the broken body and shed blood of Jesus Christ at the cross, saves us from drowning in our sins and being suffocated by God's judgment.

    A. Jonah is supposed to die in the Sea. We have earned death through disobedience also.
    Romans 6:23.

    B. Instead of the death we deserve, God has given us abundant and eternal life in Jesus Christ our Lord. John 3:16. John 8:12. John 10:10. Ephesians 3:20.

Chapter 5 – Jonah 2:1-7

1. Then Jonah prayed unto the Lord his God out of the fish's belly. 2. And said, I cried by reason of mine affliction unto the Lord; and he heard me; out of the belly of hell cried I , and thou heardest my voice. 3. For thou hadst cast me into the deep, in the midst of the seas; and the floods compassed me about: all thy billows and thy waves passed over me. 4. Then I said, I am cast out of thy sight; yet I will look again toward thy holy temple. 5. The waters compassed me about, even to the soul: the depth closed me round about, the weeds were wrapped about my head. 6. I went down to the bottoms of the mountains; the earth with her bars was about me for ever, yet hast thou brought up my life from corruption, O Lord my God. 7. When my soul fainted within me I remembered the Lord: and my prayer came in unto thee, into thine holy temple.

In these powerful verses, we are reminded about the power of prayer. These are some of the most powerful verses in the Book of Jonah, and they are among some of the most beautiful Scriptures in the entire Bible. We see here that we can call on God when we are in trouble. The Psalmist celebrates this in Psalm 46:1-3 where he states:

> God is our refuge and strength, a very present help in trouble. Therefore will not we fear, though the earth be removed, and though the mountains be carried into the midst of the sea; though the waters thereof roar and be troubled; though the mountains shake with the swelling thereof. Selah.

The Psalmist is asserting that even if mountains fall into the sea, and a tsunami overcomes us, God will still be with us to help us and bring us through. Certainly, cataclysmic events have besieged the prophet Jonah, and he has been swallowed by a huge fish. However, God is still in control, and Jonah continues to have access to his God through prayer and faith.

Even though Jonah is responsible for the terrifying events he is going through, God's grace continues to be greater than Jonah's sins. Jonah goes to God in prayer, and he longs to be with God in God's sanctuary. I've always found this particular chapter in Jonah to be most fascinating and beautiful. In this passage, we continue to see the prophet Jonah, the man of God, who loves his God and longs to be near God. Notice that Jonah refers to his present predicament and situation as "...the belly of hell..." (V. 2) In Verses 2-3, we read:

> ...I cried by reason of mine affliction unto the Lord, and he heard me: out of the belly of hell cried I, and thou heardest my voice. For thou hadst cast me into the deep, in the midst of the

> seas; and the floods compassed me about: all thy billows and thy waves passed over me.

Here, Jonah shines as a man of God should. He is not having a hellish experience because of the foul odor, lack of oxygen, threat of drowning, and the high chance of physical death he is facing. No, Jonah is experiencing the very dark valley of feeling separated from the God he loves. When we blatantly disobey God, and we refuse to obey him and run away from him, he sometimes will allow us to feel like he has abandoned us. He has not abandoned us, but the sin or the idol that we have put before God, obscures our view of God, and interrupts our sweet fellowship with him. Nothing is worth enduring the dark and desperate feeling of being separated from God.

Experiencing the Hand of God

We have a very vivid description of the agony Jonah encountered in the belly of the whale. I've always been struck by the precise detail given in Chapter 2. We read about how "…the billows and… waves passed over…"

(V. 3) him, and we read how "...the weeds were wrapped..." (V. 5) around Jonah's head. This reminds us of how in tune Jonah is with his God. When we are in tune with God, and we are accustomed to walking in humility and holiness with God, we can easily detect when the hand of God moves in our lives. Jonah is a man of God, a Jew, and a prophet, and he easily recognizes when God moves in his life. This speaks to Jonah's holiness and righteousness. In this, we see who Jonah really is. Oftentimes, in dark periods of disobedience in our lives, we vividly remember how God came to us, disciplined us, corrected us, and called us to repent and return to him. We remember the specifics just as Jonah remembers the billows, the waves, and the weeds. We remember how God came to us, and we remember how he, in his amazing grace, corrected us, called us, and put us back on the paths of righteousness (Psalm 23:3) and in that narrow way (Matthew 7:13-14) which leads to life, joy, and peace.

Discipline, Correction, and the House of the Lord

When secular and unbelieving men and women speak of our God as a judge who imposes rules and demands obedience, we have the experience of his gracious mercy, his compassionate love, his wonderful forgiveness, and his amazing grace to share with them that God is a God who loves us and them so much that he forgives us all of our sins and paid our sin debt with the broken body and shed blood of his only-begotten Son, Jesus the Christ. Like Jonah, we Christians know that our loving God has loved us much and forgiven us much, and he is worthy of all we can give him in worship, service, devotion, adoration, and praise. When he was dealing with the consequences of his sins and facing imminent death in the belly of the whale, Jonah didn't long for alcohol or drugs, and he didn't long for fine dining or a fancy vacation. He didn't long for a nice house or a fancy car. No, Jonah, in his time of trial, didn't long for any of these worldly things. He longed for his God and God's sanctuary, and he was able to immediately find God and his sanctuary by bowing his head in prayer. In Verse 7, we read:

"When my soul fainted within me I remembered the Lord: and my prayer came in unto thee, into thine holy temple." Jonah didn't turn to anything this world has to offer in his time of need. He turned to God and the church. These horrific events brought home to him the truth that our true joy and happiness is found with our Father and in our Father's house with our sisters and brothers in Christ. That's why we can celebrate the truth proclaimed by the Psalmist in Psalm 122:1 where he states: "I was glad when they said unto me, Let us go into the house of the Lord."

Prayer and the Faithfulness of God

One of the primary themes in the Book of Jonah is the faithfulness of God. In the story of Jonah, we consistently see the amazing grace of God, the faithfulness of God, and the extraordinary means that God will go to to reconcile sinners to himself. The storm, though terrifying and scary, arises from God's grace and faithfulness, and the great fish, which carries Jonah to safety, also arises from God's amazing grace and faithfulness. This reminds us that God never leaves or forsakes us, and he remains faithful even when we are unfaithful. (Hebrews 13:5; 2 Timothy 2:13) Although Jonah has blatantly disobeyed God and ran away from God, God still works through these extraordinary events to bring Jonah to safety and to give him another chance to preach to the people of Nineveh. God continues to give sinners second chances, and he is willing to go to great extremes in order to make this happen. This is seen most vividly at the cross where God, incarnate in the Jewish flesh of Jesus, bleeds and dies in order to reconcile sinners to himself. Commenting on the atoning work of Jesus at the cross, the apostle Paul proclaims "…that God was in Christ, reconciling the world unto himself, not imputing their trespasses unto them…" (2 Corinthians 5:19). God's great love for sinners, and his willingness to go to great extremes to reconcile sinners to himself, is evident in the storm and the great fish which swallows Jonah. It is also evident in the storm of the first Good Friday and in the crucifixion and resurrection of our Lord and Savior, Jesus Christ,

Chapter 6 – Jonah 2:8-10

8. They that observe lying vanities forsake their own mercy. 9. But I will sacrifice unto thee with the voice of thanksgiving; I will pay that that I have vowed. Salvation is of the Lord. 10. And the Lord spake unto the fish, and it vomited out Jonah upon the dry land.

Giving, Sacrifice, and Thanksgiving

In the midst of his trial, Jonah makes commitments to the Lord. In Verse 9, Jonah says "...I will sacrifice unto thee with the voice of thanksgiving; I will pay that that I have vowed. Salvation is of the Lord." Here, Jonah remembers the vows he had taken as a religious Jew, and he promises to keep his vows in the future. Notice, this is before God speaks to the fish and Jonah is delivered to dry land. This points out that Jonah's promises to make sacrifices with thanksgiving to God is in response to God's grace and faithfulness prior to the events in the Book of Jonah. God is worthy of sacrifices of praise and thanksgiving even if Jonah perishes in the belly of the whale in the depths of the sea.

This reminds us that we should not wait until we are in a dire situation to offer God prayers, praise, and thanksgiving for his great faithfulness to us. Those who only call upon God and make promises to God in difficult times are guilty of having what we sometimes refer to as "spare tire religion." It is as if their Christianity and spirituality are merely a "spare tire" that they only bring out when life gives them a "flat." This passage in Jonah, and the entire story of Jonah, reminds us that God is always good, and he is always worthy of worship, praise, and thanksgiving.

As devout Christians, we recognize that regardless of what we may face today or tomorrow, God has already demonstrated his great love and faithfulness to us in the life, ministry, teachings, death, and resurrection of our Lord and Savior, Jesus Christ. By the time you finish reading this sentence, God will have blessed you numerous more times with your eyes that read, your mind that comprehends the words on the page, the breaths that you breathe, and the education you received that enables you to read. God is always blessing us, and God is always good. Let us not wait until we encounter turbulent times to make promises to God and to offer prayers of thanksgiving. Turbulent times will come and go, and God promises to be with us in them all. God has proven his great love for us at the cross as St. Paul declares in Romans 5:8 where he states: "...God commendeth his love toward us, in that, while we were yet sinners, Christ died for us." And, God promises to always be with us as the Psalmist declares in Psalm 23:4 where he proclaims: "Yea, though I walk through the valley of the shadow of death, I will fear no evil: for thou art with me; thy rod and thy staff they comfort me."

The Voice of the Lord

In Verse 10, we read "And the Lord spake unto the fish, and it vomited out Jonah upon the dry land." This is a very powerful verse. In this verse, we are reminded that when God speaks, things happen. God speaks to the fish, and he instructs the fish to deliver Jonah to safety. The entire universe obeys the Voice of the Lord, and this reminds us that God can remedy any situation and deliver us from any trial just by speaking the Word. We are also reminded that God continues to speak in and through our circumstances and events in our lives, and he is with us when we face difficulties and trials.

We are never in a circumstance where God cannot rescue us. He only has to say the Word, and we will be delivered. God created the heavens and the earth by speaking, and he recreates and makes all things new by speaking also. In this passage, he speaks to the fish, and the fish responds by delivering Jonah to dry land. From this sandy beach, the minor prophet Jonah begins a new chapter in his life. He has a second chance to obey the Lord and to go and preach to the people of Nineveh. God continues to show up in our lives, and God continues to speak. As he does, we are reminded that: "…if any man be in Christ, he is a new creature: old things are passed away; behold, all things are become new" (2 Corinthians 5:17). God speaks and Jonah gets a second chance. God continues to speak, and we are given another opportunity to accomplish something great for God.

Let us not take our second chances for granted. It is a wonderful thing to have another chance to walk and talk with God and to do his will in our lives. The greatest sacrifice of praise that we can make to God is the living sacrifice of living in obedience to his Commandments and answering his call on our lives. (Romans 12:1-2) This is the second chance that Jonah is given, and he seizes upon his second chance and goes to Nineveh. We should make the most of our second chances also, and we should live our lives in obedience to God. This is where the joy and peace is found in the Christian life. It is found in obeying the Great Commandments of our Lord which are that we love God and each other. (Matthew 22:34-40; John 13:34-35) Jonah finds much misery and frustration because he refuses to love the Ninevites, and he is slow to learn that hatred brings misery into our lives while love brings us hope, joy, and peace.

Sermon Outline #2 – Jonah 2:1-10

Title: The Power of Prayer and Worship.
Theme: We have direct access to the presence and power of God through the Word, Prayer, and the Church.

1. Verse 1 – From the belly of the fish, Jonah immediately turns to God in prayer.

    A. Jonah ran from God, but God is right there when Jonah turns to him in prayer.
    B. Matthew 7:7 – God is faithful. When we ask, he gives. When we seek, we find. When we knock, God opens the door for us..

2. Verses 7-8 – While in agony, and suffering the consequences of his sins and disobedience, Jonah longs for God and the church. He misses the joy and peace, and the close fellowship with God, that is enjoyed by those who obey and walk with God.

    A. Luke 15:11-32. Like the Prodigal Son, Jonah has encountered severe difficulties due to his disobedience.
    B. Luke 15:11-32. Like the Prodigal Son, Jonah longs for his Father's house, and Jonah turns his eyes toward his Father's house.

3. Verses 9-10 – Jonah gives thanks to God and makes a commitment to live for God.

    A. When Jonah learns his lesson, God speaks to the fish, and Jonah is "delivered" from the belly of the great fish.
    B. When Jesus rose from the dead on the third day, he "delivered" all who trust in him from sin, death, and the grave. John 3:16. John 14:19.

Chapter 7 – Jonah 3:1-4

1.And the word of the Lord came unto Jonah the second time, saying, 2. Arise, go unto Nineveh, that great city, and preach unto it the preaching that I bid thee. 3. So Jonah arose, and went unto Nineveh, according to the word of the Lord. Now Nineveh was an exceeding great city of three days' journey. 4. And Jonah began to enter into the city a days journey, and he cried, and said. Yet forty days, and Nineveh shall be overthrown.

Amazing Grace and Second Chances

Here, we once again see the primacy of the Word of God as we are told in Verse 1 that "…the word of the Lord came unto Jonah the second time,…" Through the Bible, God comes to us and gives us second, third, and fourth and fifth chances. Our God is a loving, forgiving, and merciful God, and his grace is amazing. When God gives us another chance to obey him, we should seize the opportunity and be even more dedicated to obeying God in the future. The word that comes to Jonah the second time instructs him to: "Arise, go unto Nineveh, that great city, and preach unto it the preaching that I bid thee" (V. 2). As we discussed earlier, Jonah now has the choice to "arise to obedience" or to "arise to disobedience." This time, Jonah makes the correct choice, and he "arises to obey" God.

One of the things we want to continually remind ourselves of as we look at the Book of Jonah is the importance of listening to and obeying God the first time. God has given us his Word, his Commandments, and Jesus has given us the Great Commandments. Christian discipleship is not complicated. We simply stay close to God in prayer, worship, and the study of Scripture, and we consistently love God and each other. As we do this month after month, and year after year, we grow in Sanctifying Grace, and we become holier men and women of God. In the Christian life, there are some things that Christianity teaches that we were aware of even before we became Christians. One of them is that we should learn from our mistakes. God is merciful, and he is willing to forgive sin. However, as we grow in Sanctifying Grace, and we become more and more like Jesus, we learn how to resist temptation and how to defeat the enemy when he comes around with his same old bag of tricks.

We eventually learn that sin is not what we want. On the contrary, we want God, and his Word, and his Kingdom, and we find true joy and peace through walking and talking with him. Eventually, this results in us not giving in to temptation, and we are able to say "no" to the enemy and "yes" to God. This is the victory that Jesus gives us over the power and presence of sin, and it is what the apostle John speaks of in 1 John 1:7 where he states: "…if we walk in the light, as he is in the light, we have fellowship one with another, and the blood of Jesus Christ his Son cleanseth us from all sin." Our victory over the power and presence of sin in our lives inspires us and gives us even more incentive to resist temptation when it comes our way. We are unwilling to give up any of the progress we have made as Christians, and we begin to realize the importance of keeping God first and obeying God the first time he speaks. The result of obeying God the first time he speaks is more joy and peace in our lives, and less frustration, as God blesses us for our obedience, and doesn't have to discipline us for our disobedience.

Jonah's Gift and Preaching Ministry

This time, Jonah "arises to obedience," and he goes to Nineveh. In Verse 2, we read that God has given Jonah the gift of preaching his Word. In Verse 2, God says to Jonah: "Arise, go unto Nineveh, that great city, and preach unto it the preaching that I bid thee." Here, God makes it very clear that he will reveal to Jonah the messages he is to preach to the people of Nineveh. This reminds us that God doesn't necessarily call the qualified, but he qualifies the called. If God calls us to do something, he will also empower, enable, and equip us to accomplish the task. This is tied in with God's amazing grace and great faithfulness which are pervasive themes in the Book of Jonah. If God were to call us or command us to accomplish something, but not give us the talents and abilities to accomplish the work, this would not be consistent with God's character and faithfulness. God calls Jonah to go and preach to the Ninevites, and he calls Jonah a second time to go and preach to the Ninevites. God's grace and faithfulness are seen in the fact that Jonah gets a second chance to answer the call and also in the fact that God promises to give him the messages he is to preach to the inhabitants of the city.

Jonah Warns the Inhabitants of Nineveh

Now, in Verse 4, we read that "...Jonah began to enter into the city a day's journey, and he cried, and said, Yet forty days, and Nineveh shall be overthrown." God gives Jonah the message that Nineveh will be overthrown for sinning against God unless they repent and turn to the Lord. We see here that God loves and cares about the Ninevites, and we are reminded that God oftentimes warns sinners and gives them the opportunity to change their ways before he lowers his wrath upon them. The people of Nineveh are a very sinful people, and this is probably why Jonah doesn't like them. Jonah ran from the first call to go to Nineveh primarily because he didn't like the Ninevites. This brings home the fact that God loves and cares for all people, and this includes those we "religious folk" consider to be sinners and outside the realm of respectability.

The entire Book of Luke, and several other places in the Scriptures, deal with the fact that God loves sinners and outsiders, and we who follow Christ are called to care for and love sinners and outsiders as well. Indeed, in the Parable of the Last Judgment in Matthew 25:31-46, Jesus teaches us that we will be rewarded, and have rewards withheld, at the judgment seat of Christ (2 Corinthians 5:10) based on how we care for the hungry, the thirsty, the naked, the prisoner, and the stranger. In this Parable, Jesus plainly states: "…Inasmuch as ye have done it unto one of the least of these my brethren, ye have done it unto me" (Matthew 25:40). At the judgment seat of Christ, Jesus will determine how much we love him by how much we loved one another, and the least of these, during our time here on earth.

When we choose hatred instead of love, we are fooling ourselves if we think that God will not send a storm and something to swallow us up. He will send the storm, and allow our sin to swallow us up, because he is too faithful to let us continue in the way of sin and hatred. He calls and equips us to love him and one another, and he gives every Christian specific gifts to be used for his glory, the expansion of his kingdom, and the edification and building up of his church. When given the second chance to answer God's call and to obey God, Jonah "arises to obey" God, and he goes to Nineveh. He preaches the messages that God faithfully gives him, and he warns the Ninevites that judgment is coming unless they repent and turn away from their sins. God loves Jonah, and he loves the Ninevites. He expects Jonah to love them also just as he expects us to love others as he has first loved us. The apostle John sums this up succinctly in 1 John 4:11 where he states: "Beloved, if God so loved us, we ought also to love one another."

In the great mercy God shows to both Jonah and the Ninevites, we see God's amazing grace and faithfulness, and we see his great love for sinners. The three parables of Luke

15 point out how God loves and forgives sinners and how God is displeased with those who are self-righteous and have a sense of religious superiority. As a Hebrew prophet, Jonah looked down on the Ninevites with disdain and contempt. By doing this, he was sinning against his God and not reflecting his God's love for all of humanity. God rejoices when sinners repent and return to him, and we Christians should rejoice also because we are told in Luke 15:10 that "…there is joy in the presence of the angels of God over one sinner that repenteth."

Chapter 8 – Jonah 3:5-10

5. So the people of Nineveh believed God, and proclaimed a fast, and put on sackcloth, from the greatest of them even to the least of them. 6. For word came unto the king of Nineveh, and he arose from his throne, and he laid his robe from him, and covered him with sackcloth, and sat in ashes. 7. And he caused it to be proclaimed and published through Nineveh by the decree of the king and his nobles, saying, Let neither man nor beast, herd nor flock, taste any thing; let them not feed, nor drink water; 8. But let man and beast be covered with sackcloth, and cry mightily unto God; yea, let them turn every one from his evil way, and from the violence that is in their hands. 9. Who can tell if God will turn and repent, and turn away from his fierce anger, that we perish not? 10. And God saw their works, and they turned from their evil way; and God repented of the evil, that he had said that he would do unto them; and he did it not.

Jonah's Ministry Bears Fruit

Since he "arises to obey" God this time, Jonah's goes to Nineveh, and his preaching bears much fruit. When we obey the teachings of Christ in all areas of our lives, we receive favor from God, and he blesses our work and ministries. This is not always the case because God sometimes works in ways that are very mysterious and foreign to us, but, for the most part, God blesses obedience and disciplines disobedience. When we are Baptized, and we become card-carrying members of the church, God makes a covenant to be with us in our lives and ministries. God's presence and power in our lives and ministries is made possible in and through the Holy Spirit who is the Third Person of the Holy Trinity. As we walk by faith and obey the Great Commandments of Christ by loving God and each other, we grow in Sanctifying Grace and holiness. Occasionally, we will sense those powerful words that were heard when John the Baptist Baptized Jesus: "…'This is my beloved [son, daughter], in whom I am well pleased.'" (Matthew 3:17)

Indeed, these words apply to Jonah as he goes into Nineveh. He preaches the messages God gives him, and he bears much fruit as the king and the people of Nineveh repent and turn from their sins and turn to God. In Verse 5, we read: "So the people of Nineveh believed God, and proclaimed a fast, and put on sackcloth, from the greatest of them even to the least of them." In Jonah's sermons, God warns the Ninevites that they will be overthrown within forty days, and the Ninevites hear the Voice of the Lord in Jonah's sermons. They repent of their sins, begin fasting, and put on sackcloth as outward symbols of their inward contrition and repentance. This reminds us that we preachers can effect great change through our preaching and teaching ministries. Jonah's obedience in answering God's call, and preaching God's sermons, saves an entire city of over 120,000 people.

Christian ministry, when carried out by faithful disciples walking in faith and obedience, can save lives and bring about great changes in society and the world. Those of us involved in Christian ministry, both clergy and laity, need to remember that we are the ones with the beautiful feet who bring life, hope, and peace to places of sadness, desperation, and pain. We are the ones Isaiah speaks of in Isaiah 52:7 where he proclaims: "How beautiful upon the mountains are the feet of him that bringeth good tidings, that publisheth peace, that bringeth good tidings of good, that publisheth salvation; that saith unto Zion, Thy God reigneth!" Indeed, Jonah's feet are among the beautiful feet of those who bring the good news that God will show mercy if the Ninevites repent and turn to God. The Ninevites receive the Word of the Lord, and they repent and are spared. The Ninevites are given a second chance from Jonah's God who gives second, third, and three hundred thirty-third chances to those who turn from their sins and trust in his unfailing mercy and amazing grace.

Nineveh Repents and God Changes His Mind

The Ninevites repent in response to the sermons God gives to Jonah to preach. Those of us who have been called to preach, teach, and prophesy celebrate the truth contained here that God will give us the messages we are to preach. God is with us in our ministries, and he promises us that his Word is always effective. Along these lines, God tells us through Isaiah: "So shall my word be that goeth forth out of my mouth; it shall not return unto me void, but it shall accomplish that which I please, and it shall prosper in the thing whereto I sent it" (Isaiah 55:11). God reminds us in the story of Jonah that his Word, which he sends to the Ninevites through the preaching ministry of the prophet Jonah, cannot be stopped. This is related to God's great faithfulness and his amazing grace and mercy. God refuses to give up on the Ninevites, and he refuses to give up on Jonah. When Jonah disobeys God's Word the first time, God sends his Word to Jonah a second time. Having learned from his mistakes, Jonah obeys the Word that comes to him the second time. He goes to Nineveh, and he preaches the messages God gives him. Through Jonah's oracles and teachings, God warns the people of Nineveh that they will encounter serious consequences if they do not heed the warning and repent of their sins.

Some may be tempted to see God as being merciless and uncaring in the "warning" aspect of Jonah's preaching. However, the "warnings" are just that. God is "warning" the Ninevites instead of "threatening" them, and God does this because he is a God of love, compassion, and mercy. He wants to forgive the Ninevites for their sins because he is a God who celebrates when sinners repent. (See Luke 15) In the Parable of the Lost Sheep, Jesus teaches us that God is like the shepherd who rejoices when he finds the one sheep he lost, and Jesus says:

> And when he cometh, he calleth together his friends and neighbours, saying unto them, Rejoice with me; for I have found my sheep which was lost. I say unto you that likewise joy shall be in heaven over one sinner that repenteth, more than over ninety and nine just persons, which need no repentance.
> (Luke 15:6-7)

God rejoices and celebrates when sinners repent of their sins and turn to him in faith. He celebrates when sinners turn from their sins and make a commitment to live for and walk with God.

The story of Jonah reminds us preachers and Evangelical Christians that God loves the ungodly, and he calls us to witness to them and to offer them Christ. As Christians, we are simply not allowed to categorize some persons as "off limits" or "beyond" the grace of God. Unless we like being thrown in oceans, and being swallowed huge and hungry fish or other animals, we may want to learn the lesson that Jonah had to learn the hard way. We bear witness to and offer Christ to all persons because God loves, and Jesus died and arose again, for "whosoever" believes in him. (John 3:16) St. Paul reminds us that God loves and Jesus died for the ungodly by declaring: "For when we were yet without strength, in due time Christ died for the ungodly" (Romans 5:6). God loves and calls us to preach and witness to the vilest of sinners. We are fooling ourselves if we think we can simply overlook and ignore certain persons because of their sinfulness or because they consider themselves our enemies. God loved us, and Jesus died for us, when we were God's enemies and living sinful lives. Therefore, we only grow in holiness and become more like God and Jesus when we love others, love our enemies, and love those that society has deemed worthless and unworthy of grace and salvation. The hypocrisy of those who pick and choose who they will and will not minister to is highlighted by the apostle John who emphatically states:

> We love him, because he first loved us. If a man say, I love God, and hatheth his brother, he is a liar: for he that loveth not his brother whom he hath seen, how can he love God whom he hath not seen? And this

> commandment have we from him, That he who loveth God love his brother also.
> (1 John 4:19-21)

God did not tolerate Jonah's refusal to minister to the Ninevites, and the Word of God continued to come to Jonah until he obeyed it and went to Nineveh and preached God's messages.

Jonah's ministry in Nineveh was very fruitful, and the Word of God was received by the king and the Ninevites. The king and the people of Nineveh receive the Word of God Jonah delivers, repent of their sins, and begin fasting and wearing sackcloth as signs of their penance and contrition. They also demonstrate faith in God's mercy and compassion as we see in Verse 9 where we read: "Who can tell if God will turn and repent, and turn away from his fierce anger, that we perish not?" God blesses the ministry and preaching of Jonah now that he is receiving the Word and answering God's call. We too are blessed as we receive the Word and daily strive to do God's will and answer his call in our daily lives. Jonah didn't like the Ninevites, and he didn't want to go and preach to them. However, God was unwilling to give up on Jonah or the Ninevites, and he sends his Word to the Ninevites in the preaching ministry of Jonah. They repent of their sins, and God changes his mind about destroying them for their sins. This reminds us that repentance gets God's attention and that God recognizes and rewards repentance. Repentance changes things, and God blesses those who turn away from their sins and turn toward him with commitment, obedience, and faith.

God Sees Everything

One of the things that is great about God is that he sees everything. Now, in times of sin and disobedience, some may argue that this is somewhat disturbing and not something to celebrate. However, the fact that our loving God sees all is a magnificent truth, and those of us who have decided to spend our lives loving, knowing, and serving him celebrate this truth. He is always watching out for us, and we know that there is nowhere we can go or be taken to that his watchful eye does not watch over us. One of the great things about Christian discipleship is that God sees and honors our intentions and motivations instead of just our actions and practical results. In this "results oriented" world which emphasizes "productivity and profit," we get very little reward and recognition for our inner disposition, motivations, or intentions. However, with God, the inner motivation is extremely important and much more important than numbers, quotas, and productivity.

God blesses us for just wanting others to be blessed, for inner thoughts of love and forgiveness, and for inner contrition and poverty of spirit which results from mourning and repenting of our sins. This is why Jesus says:

> Blessed are the poor in spirit: for theirs is the kingdom of heaven. Blessed are they that mourn: for they shall be comforted.
> (Matthew 5:3-4)

God sees what's in our hearts as we read in 1 Samuel 16:7: "...the Lord seeth not as man seeth; for man looketh on the outward appearance, but the Lord looketh on the heart." God blesses us not only for what we do and accomplish but also for the good and loving thoughts, ideas, intentions, and motivations that only he can see. We see that this is true for the Ninevites following their conversion as we read in Verse 10: "And God saw their works, that they turned from their evil way; and God repented of the evil, that he had said that he would do unto them; and he did it not." God always sees and honors true and genuine repentance, and he always forgives those who forsake their sins and turn to him in obedience and faith.

Sermon Outline #3 – Jonah 3:1-10

Title: "When We Get a Second Chance"
Theme: The Power of the Word of God.

1. Verses 1-2 – The Word of God comes to Jonah a second time, and God gives Jonah a second chance. When we stay in God's Word, God opens doors for ministry and gives us second, third, and three hundred and thirty third chances

    A. Psalm 119:105 – The Word of God is a lamp that lights our way in this dark world.
    B. Isaiah 55:11 – The Word of God is powerful and effective and accomplishes that for which God sends it to accomplish.

2. Verse 5 – Jonah obeys and preaches the messages God gives him to preach to the Ninevites, and God blesses his preaching and Jonah's ministry bears fruit. When we trust God's Word, and answer God's call, God also blesses us, and our ministries bear fruit.
    A. Romans 10:17 – The Ninevites listen to Jonah.
    B. 2 Chronicles 7:14 – The Ninevites repent and turn away from their sins. Matthew 3:8. Matthew 5:4.

3. Verse 10 – God sees that the Ninevites repent of their sins, and God decides not to destroy them.
    A. God sees everything. This is a good thing when what God sees is repentance and holiness.
    B. 1 John 1:9 – If we confess our sins, and repent and turn away from our sins, God faithfully forgives us and cleanses us. Matthew 5:48.

Chapter 9 – Jonah 4:1-4

1.But it displeased Jonah exceedingly, and he was very angry. 2. And he prayed unto the Lord, and said, I pray thee, O Lord, was not this my saying, when I was yet in my country? Therefore I fled unto Tarshish: for I knew that thou art a gracious God, and merciful, slow to anger, and of great kindness, and repentest thee of the evil. 3. Therefore now, O Lord, take, I beseech thee, my life from me; for it is better for me to die than to live. 4. Then said the Lord, Doest thou well to be angry?

Jonah's Hatred and Anger

Hatred is a terrible thing, and in the church it is considered one of the seven deadly sins. Jonah hates the Ninevites, and he is angry that they have repented and received God's mercy and forgiveness. One of the main reasons Jonah fled to Tarshish is because he didn't like the Ninevites, and he didn't want to go and minister to them. This is blatant discrimination, and Jonah was guilty of the sin of racism. God has a particular disdain for persons who hate, and God is particularly offended by racism. The fact that Jonah gets angry because God shows mercy to the Ninevites demonstrates how far hatred goes into the nonsensical and absurd. Christian humility and the Great Commandments of

Christ make hatred a particularly serious sin, and racism is when the hatred is based on race, creed, color, ethnicity, or national origin. We may speculate as to why Jonah disliked the Ninevites, but the reasons are not really important when analyzing the story from a Christian perspective.

Hatred and racism are unacceptable in the life of the obedient Christian disciple. As obedient Christians, we are not only to love all other people, but we are to also love our enemies and those who hate and mistreat us. In the Sermon on the Mount, Jesus states:

> Ye have heard that it hath been said, Thou shalt love thy neighbor, and hate thine enemy. But I say unto you, Love your enemies, bless them that curse you, do good to them that hate you, and pray for them which despitefully use you, and persecute you;
> (Matthew 5:43-44)

Sometimes, we might think things would be much simpler if Jesus hadn't taught us to love even our enemies and those who persecute us. Many other religions do not require this. However, only Jesus Christ is Lord. Therefore, the born again, believing Christian disciple must find a way to love all persons, even his or her enemies. Of course, one can be saved and not obedient. However, those who are saved and not obedient miss out on the power and glory of the risen Christ in their lives and ministries, and they miss out on the joy and peace that comes from close fellowship with the Good Shepherd. Also, when obedient Christians get to the judgment seat of Christ, they receive much more reward than those who are saved by "the skin of their teeth" and barely escape eternal separation from God. Also, when we really love Jesus and are really thankful for what he did for us on the cross, we want to obey him, and we want to love God, each other, and our enemies also. Loving our enemies doesn't happen overnight. However, as we grow more mature as Christians, and we grow holier in Sanctifying Grace, we find ourselves becoming more like Christ and able to love all others including our enemies. Holiness grows and accumulates as we obey the Great Commandments of Christ day in and day out, and the Great Commandments of Christ are that we love God and each other. (Matthew 22:34-40)

Jonah Complains and Wants to Die

In the story of Jonah, we see the great lengths that hatred can take us to. Jonah is so angry that God shows mercy to the Ninevites that he blames God for the fact that they are not destroyed. And, he is so upset that they are not destroyed, that he wants to die. In Verses 2-3, we read that:

> ...he prayed unto the Lord, and said, I pray thee, O Lord, was not this my saying, when I was yet in my country? Therefore I fled unto Tarshish: for I knew that thou art a gracious God, and merciful, slow to anger, and of great kindness, and repentest thee of the evil.

Jonah's mindset demonstrates the terrible effect that hatred and racism have on the person who allows them to infest his or her heart and mind. Jonah's hatred of the Ninevites is so profound that he would just rather be dead than to see anything good happen to them.

The fact that Jonah is a religious man who knows God is evident in the fact that he knows God is a "gracious God, and merciful, slow to anger, and of great kindness,..." (V. 2). Jonah is forgiven and given a second chance because God is gracious, merciful, and kind, yet Jonah doesn't want the

Ninevites to be shown the same. Herein lies the hypocrisy of hatred and racism. It is simply unacceptable for a Christian to refuse to forgive and love any other person after having been forgiven and loved so much by God. In fact, St. John points out that those who refuse to love others are probably not saved by stating:

> We know that we have passed from death unto life, because we love the brethren. He that loveth not his brother abideth in death. Whosoever hateth his brother is a murderer: and ye know that no murderer hath eternal life abiding in him.
> (1 John 3:14-15)

This is very emphatic, and the apostle John doesn't tap dance around the truth. Christians who truly have even an impartial understanding of the un-payable debt that Christ paid for them at the cross will go to great lengths to obey God in every area of their lives, and they simply know that they are called to love and forgive others, including enemies, as God has loved and forgiven them. God recognizes their commitment to him, and God blesses them for doing things his way instead of the way of the world. God blesses us and rewards our obedience to his Son's Commandments both in this life and the next, and Jonah is missing out on these blessings by continuing to hate the Ninevites. As God's prophet and preacher, Jonah should be celebrating with God that the Ninevites have repented, turned from their sins, and begun fasting and wearing sackcloth as signs of their penance and contrition. However, the hateful heart is a selfish heart, and the hate in Jonah's heart has so negatively affected Jonah's psyche that he is fiercely angry, and wanting to die, when he should be celebrating the fruit of his preaching ministry and the grace, mercy, and kindness of his God.

The Futility of Anger and the Joy of Love

The question that God asks Jonah in Verse 4 is very interesting. In Verse 4, God asks Jonah: "…Doest thou well to be angry?" What is God asking here? He is basically asking Jonah what does he get out of hating the Ninevites so much? God is asking Jonah what incentive does he have to hate so much? Of course, the question is rhetorical in that it is very obvious that there is no rational reason for, nor is there any great gain, for Jonah's hatred. He simply hates the Ninevites because he wants to hate them, and this is how the stubborn and selfish mind of the racist works. There doesn't have to be any monetary gain or incentive to hate because the hate itself is its own reward. The sinful flesh of the sinner enjoys sin itself, and there need not be any gain, reward, or recognition associated with the hatred.

Interestingly, the same is true of love and righteousness in that they are their own reward as we are blessed by loving one another in the love alone. However, God also blesses us when we love one another just as he judges and disciplines us when we don't love one another. Along these lines, the apostle Paul points out:

> For they that are after the flesh do mind the things of the flesh; but they that are after the Spirit, the things of the Spirit. For to be carnally minded is death; but to be spiritually minded is life and peace. Because the carnal mind is enmity against God: for it is not subject to the law of God, neither indeed can be. So then they that are in the flesh cannot please God.
> (Romans 8:5-8)

Those of us who love Jesus Christ love him because he went to the cross, bled and died for us, and shed his blood to save us from our sins. We want to obey his Great Commandments, and we strive to love all persons including our enemies. We don't do it just because he commands it. We do it because we love him, and we know that we demonstrate our love for him by obeying his Commandments and loving one another. By obeying our Lord's Commandments, we grow closer in our fellowship with him and with others, and we experience peace and joy in our lives. Anger is a waste of time and energy while love is a great use of our time, talents, and resources. Love is its own reward, and obedience is its own reward, for Jesus plainly states: "If ye love me, keep my commandments" (John 14:15).

Chapter 10 – Jonah 4:5-11

5.So Jonah went out of the city, and sat on the east side of the city, and there made him a booth, and sat under it in the shadow, till he might see what would become of the city. 6. And the Lord God prepared a gourd, and made it come up over Jonah, that it might be a shadow over his head to deliver him from his grief. So Jonah was exceeding glad of the gourd. 7. But God prepared a worm when the morning rose the next day, and it smote the gourd that it withered. 8. And it came to pass, when the sun did arise, that God prepared a vehement east wind; and the sun beat upon the head of Jonah, that he fainted, and wished in himself to die, and said it is better for me to die than to live. 9. And God said to Jonah, Doest thou well to be angry for the gourd? And he said, I do well to be angry, even unto death. 10. Then said the Lord, Thou hast had pity on the gourd, for the which thou hast not labored, neither madest it grow; which came up in a night, and perished in a night: 11. And should not I spare Nineveh, that great city, wherein are more than sixscore thousand persons that cannot discern between their right hand and their left hand; and also much cattle?

Jonah Anticipates the Destruction of Nineveh

In this part of the story, we see that Jonah prepares for himself a front row seat, a booth, from which he can kick back and enjoy the show of God's judgment raining down on the Ninevites whom he despises so much. It is never acceptable for the Christian to want or will something harmful or painful on another person or people. The Christian is called to love and want the best for others including even his or her enemies or persecutors. Jonah's desire to sit in his booth and enjoy watching God destroy Nineveh comes from his pride. Pride is the primary cardinal sin, and the other six cardinal sins are all rooted in and arise from pride. We see in the Scriptures in many places that God particularly dislikes the proud. In James 4:6, we read that: "…God resisteth the proud, but giveth grace unto the humble." In Proverbs 6:16-19, we have a list of "…six things doth the Lord hate…" and "…a proud look…" is the first thing listed. The fact that God goes out of his way to bring down the proud is highlighted in Mary's Magnificat as our Lord's mother proclaims:

> He hath shewed strength with his arm; he hath scattered the proud in the imagination of their hearts. He hath put down the mighty from their seats, and exalted them of low degree. He hath filled the hungry with good things; and the rich he hath sent empty away.
> (Luke 1:51-53)

Jonah's racism is rooted in his pride, and his eager anticipation of watching Nineveh's destruction from his comfortable booth is rooted in his pride also. This behavior is simply unacceptable.

As Christians, who have been called and commanded to love God and all others, it is never acceptable to want or to will something negative, painful, or destructive on other individuals or groups of people. The law of Christianity is love as St. Paul states in Galatians 5:14 where we read: "For all the law is fulfilled in one word, even in this; Thou shalt love thy neighbor as thyself." The Scriptures are clear that the proud set themselves up in a position opposite to God and in opposition to God, and God has a way of winning every time sinful men and women take a stand against him. Jonah proudly and defiantly takes his front row seat to see the "feature presentation" of God destroying Nineveh. However, Nineveh is not to be destroyed because they have humbled themselves, repented of their sins, and turn to God in faith and obedience. Jonah is the one who once again needs to be humbled and brought down from his pedestal from whence he looks down on and longs for the destruction of the Ninevites.

God Prepares a Gourd, a Worm, and a Wind

As Jonah settles in in his booth that he made, God prepares a gourd to arise in order to shade Jonah's head from the warm rays of the Sun. Notice in Verse 5 that Jonah built the booth because God never takes part in the sinful and proud part of sinful man that gloats and celebrates when those he doesn't like face difficulties. The booth is the front row seat Jonah reserves in his pride and hatred to enjoy watching the calamities he expects to come upon Nineveh. God does not take part in such evil and wickedness, so Jonah makes the booth with no help and no support from God. God does not support or help, or stand beside, the racist who proudly refuses to obey God's Commandments that we love God and each other. Jonah prepares the booth which arises from his disobedience, unfaithfulness, and hatred. However, God prepares a gourd, a worm, and a wind which arise from his enduring mercy, great faithfulness, and amazing grace and love.

Here, we see that Jonah is once again in a state of disobedience as he wants and wills the destruction of Nineveh. And, once again, we see that God's amazing grace and great faithfulness are seen in the fact that he works through and orchestrates events to get Jonah back into his will. This chapter of the Book of Jonah shows us how God is at work even in the minor events in our lives, and he works in and through even the small things and events, in our lives and ministries, that we sometimes think are irrelevant or unimportant. We see this here in Jonah's story as God's grace comes to Jonah through the gourd, the worm, and the east wind.

In Verses 6-8, we read that:

> And the Lord God prepared a gourd, and made it come up over Jonah, that it might be a shadow over his head to deliver him from his grief. So Jonah was exceeding glad of the gourd. But God prepared a worm when the morning rose the next day, and it smote the gourd that it withered. And it came to pass,

when the sun did arise, that God prepared a vehement east wind, and the sun beat upon the head of Jonah, that he fainted, and wished in himself to die, and said, It is better for me to die than to live.

While Jonah settles in to view and celebrate the destruction of Nineveh, we see that God is working and orchestrating events in order to bring Jonah back into a state of obedience. By preparing to gloat over and enjoy the destruction of Nineveh, Jonah is breaking both of the Great Commandments. He is not loving God because he is not celebrating God's grace and mercy shown to the Ninevites, and he is not loving his neighbors because he wants Nineveh to be destroyed instead of saved. Nevertheless, God doesn't give up on Jonah. On the contrary, God continues to work through even the smallest aspects of Jonah's life and ministry in order to bring Jonah back in line with his will.

In Verse 5, we see that Jonah built and erected the booth in order for it to provide shade for him from the sun. However, it was evidently ineffective. This reminds us that the preparations we try to make without God's help, and outside of God's will, are frequently futile and ineffective. Remember, the entire purpose of the booth was for it to be a comfortable front row seat for Jonah to occupy while he enjoyed watching the destruction of Nineveh. This reminds us that we cannot expect God to help us accomplish things, and for things to work well, when we are disobeying the Great Commandments of our Lord. This is what Jesus speaks of in John 15:4 where he says: "Abide in me, and I in you. As the branch cannot bear fruit of itself, except it abide in the vine; no more can ye, except ye abide in me." In his state of disobedience, awaiting the "feature presentation" of the destruction of Nineveh, Jonah cannot expect God to help him build a booth for this purpose. When we will and want negative things on others, we are disobeying God and breaking the Great Commandments of our Lord. The things we attempt from this type of egocentric, self-centered, motivation will not bring us joy and peace, and we cannot expect God to assist us in these sinful pursuits. On the contrary, God will be working behind the scenes to bring us out of the place of disobedience just as he works through the gourd, the worm, and the wind to put Jonah back on the right track. This is what the Psalmist speaks of in Psalm 23:3 where he proclaims: "He restoreth my soul: he leadeth me in the paths of righteousness for his name's sake."

Because God loves Jonah, and doesn't want Jonah to be out of his will, he makes the booth ineffective. Jonah is uncomfortable in the hot sun, so God sends a gourd to provide shade for Jonah. The gourd, the worm, and the east wind all arise from God's grace just as the inefficiency of the booth is rooted and grounded in God's grace. Sometimes, God's grace is found when our plans and schemes fail. God sends the gourd to provide shade for Jonah even though Jonah is once again being disobedient. This reminds us that God still loves us and cares for us even when we disobey him and sin. However, we see that God not only still loves us, but he loves us so much that he works through events to bring us back into fellowship with him.

Jonah celebrates the arrival of the gourd because it provides shade and makes him more comfortable. However, the next morning God sends a worm that invades the gourd and destroys it. God also sends an east wind which joins the sun in making Jonah increasingly uncomfortable. Jonah is so upset over the demise of the gourd that he once again wants to die. We see here how sin warps our perspective and distorts how we interpret reality. Jonah doesn't recognize that he wouldn't even be in this situation were it not for him wanting to kick back and watch God destroy Nineveh. His willing and wanting calamity to come upon the Ninevites is the only reason he is sitting in this silly little booth, in the heat of the sun, and being pounded by the wind. Jonah has become a slave to his sin of hatred and his racism, and his sin requires him to build an ineffective booth and to sit in the sun and wind. Here, we see what Jesus speaks of in John 8:34 where he says: "...Verily, verily, I say unto you, Whosoever commiteth sin is the servant of sin." In his disobedience, Jonah is a servant to his sin. God works through these events to bring Jonah back into the way of righteousness.

The fact that we are not to serve sin, but we are to serve righteousness, is emphasized by the apostle Paul who proclaims:

> Know ye not, that to whom ye yield yourselves servants to obey, his servants ye are to whom ye obey; whether of sin unto death, or of obedience unto righteousness? But God be thanked, that ye were the servants of sin, but ye have obeyed from the heart that form of doctrine which was delivered you. Being then made free from sin, ye became the servants of righteousness.
> (Romans 6:16-18)

The Scriptures make it very clear that we either live for God or we don't. There is very little "gray" area, and when we ride the fence, we are probably being disobedient. Also, when we refuse to decide and stand for what is right, our refusal to decide is in itself a decision that oftentimes puts us in the position of being disobedient. Jonah still despises the Ninevites, and he still doesn't want them to receive mercy and forgiveness. Even after being saved from the middle of the ocean and the belly of a whale, receiving so much grace and forgiveness himself, Jonah still wants Nineveh to be judged harshly for their sins. This is obviously hypocrisy, and it reminds us that those of us who have been loved and forgiven much should also want others to be loved and forgiven much. This is what Jesus speaks of when he says: "...For unto whomsoever much is given, of him shall be much required..." (Luke 12:48)

Jonah Wants to Die and the Ninevites Live

Jonah is so angry about the demise of the gourd that he once again wants to die. Once again, this demonstrates the power and destructive nature of hatred and racism. By choosing hatred and sin, Jonah chooses death. His hatred of the Ninevites is so profound that he would rather die than to see them forgiven. However, he grieves the death of a plant, the gourd, because it was important to him. The gourd provided Jonah shade from the hot sun, so it is important and valuable to him. The Ninevites, however, are not worth anything to Jonah because he hates them and sees no good in them. This is the warped perspective and distorted view of the racist. The racist may love his or her family, friends, animals, plants, and even material things and objects, yet he or she refuses to love whole groups of human beings who have been created in the image of God. Obviously, such a perspective is pure sin and wickedness and not in line with the teachings and the Great Commandments of Christ.

In Verses 10-11, God challenges Jonah's warped and distorted perspective by declaring:

> ...Thou hast had pity on the gourd, for the which thou hast not labored, neither madest it grow; which came up in a night, and perished in a night: And should not I spare Nineveh, that great city, wherein are more than six-score thousand persons that cannot discern between their right hand and their left hand; and also much cattle?

Jonah cares about and grieves the death of a gourd, but he had prepared a front row seat in order to enjoy watching the destruction of 120,000 men, women, and children. This reminds us of just how destructive and corrosive hatred and racism can be. It has the capability of taking over and overriding all logic and common sense. Jonah mourns the death of a plant yet could care less about the possible deaths of all the people of Nineveh. Once again, Jonah is being less than he should be, and he is not behaving in a way consistent with the Hebrew prophet God has called and qualified him to be.

Notice, God points out the fact that Jonah did nothing to bring about the arrival of the gourd, but he grieves and is angered at its demise. On the contrary, Jonah finally obeyed God, went to Nineveh, preached to the Ninevites, and the people of Nineveh are converted as God works in and through the ministry of Jonah. However, Jonah still wants to see them destroyed. His hatred has him unable to even enjoy and celebrate the fruits of his own ministry. Because hatred can be so poisonous and destructive, God prohibits it in the Sixth Commandment which is: "Thou shalt not kill" (Exodus 20:13). Although the Sixth Commandment literally prohibits murder, the meaning and intention of the Sixth Commandment is "Thou shalt not hate."

As Christians, Jesus taught us that we are held accountable to not just the letter of the Ten Commandments, but we are expected to honor and obey the spirit of the Ten Commandments also. A Jew or a Pharisee could obey the Sixth Commandment by simply not murdering others. However, we Christians only obey the Sixth Commandment when we not only don't murder others, but we refuse to hate others also. Jesus clearly teaches this in the Sermon on the Mount where he states:

> …except your righteousness shall exceed the righteousness of the scribe and the Pharisees, ye shall in no case enter into the kingdom of heaven. Ye have heard that it was said by them of old time. Thou shalt not kill; and whosoever shall kill shall be in danger of the judgment: But I say unto you, That whosoever is angry with his brother without a cause shall be in danger of the judgment: and whosoever shall say to his brother, Raca, shall be in danger of the council: but whosoever shall say, Thou fool, shall be in danger of hell fire.
> (Matthew 5:20-22)

Interestingly, our Lord denounces calling others derogatory names which is something racists often do. It can be no more clear that hatred is a very serious sin which brings the judgment, corrective discipline, and chastening of God. Jonah's story reminds us of the importance of obeying the Great Commandments of our Lord by loving God and loving others.

As Christians, we are to love and forgive as God has loved and forgiven us. As we consistently do this, we grow in Sanctifying Grace, and we actually become more loving and more like God. Hatred and sin, however, take us backwards in the opposite direction of God and his amazing grace and love. Jonah kept trying to go backwards instead of moving forward with God as God brought salvation to the people of Nineveh. As we obey the Great Commandments of Christ, we can know that we are moving forward and growing in grace as we love God and one another. Jesus makes it clear that persons will know we are Christians by our love by declaring:

> A new commandment I give unto you, That ye love one another; as I have loved you, that ye also love one another. By this shall all men

> know that ye are my disciples, if ye have love one to another.
> (John 13:34-35)

We see throughout the Scriptures, and the teachings of our Lord, that God is always on the side of love. By consistently hating the Ninevites, Jonah kept putting himself in opposition to God so God needed to discipline and correct him. As a religious man and a Hebrew prophet, Jonah should have known better than to hate the Ninevites. His story is still here, hundreds of years later, to remind us to choose love and not hate, and to choose righteousness and not sin, so that we can be the best we can be for God. As we do this consistently, we do what Jesus speaks of in Matthew 5:16 where he says: "Let your light so shine before men, that they may see your good works, and glorify your Father which is in heaven."

Sermon Outline #4 – Jonah 4:1-11

Title: "When We Are Not Glad That God Is Good"
Theme: God's great love for and willingness to forgive sinners.

1. Verses 1-3 – Jonah hates the Ninevites so much that, when they repent and are forgiven, Jonah becomes angry and wants to die.

   A. Exodus 20:13 -- The Sixth Commandment – You shall not hate.
   B. Matthew 5:43-45 – Love your enemies.

2. Verses 6-8 – Jonah selfishly loves a plant, because it benefits him, but he could care less about 120,000 Ninevites.

   A. John 8:34 -- Sin enslaves us and warps our perspective.
   B. John 8:36 – In Christ, we are freed from hatred and sin, and we are empowered to love. John 13:34-35.

3. Verses 10-11 – God encourages Jonah to celebrate the salvation of the Ninevites. Jonah preached to the Ninevites, and he should be happy that they responded to his messages with repentance, faith, and good works.

   A. Luke 15:7 – God rejoices when sinners repent.
   B. 1 John 4:19-21. Matthew 22:34-40 – Those who love God must love their neighbors also. The Great Commandments of our Lord are that we love God and each other.

Made in the USA
Columbia, SC
20 November 2021